LIAM
THE LONESOME
LIBRARY BOOK

By

Bob Vogel & Debbie Ciocca

Dedication

To our grandchildren: Benjamin Vogel,

Hayden Stokes and Natalie and Valerie Ciocca,

who bring joy and happiness into our lives.

Acknowledgments

We would like to thank our family and friends for their unwavering support throughout our project. We would also like to thank DeShonna Cauley for her insightful feedback on our illustrations.

We would like to thank Tom Goodman, our Project Manager, Lauren Rogers, our Illustrator, and Ian Murray, our Formatter at Amazon Publishing for all of their hard work in helping us get our book published. A very special thank you goes out to Liam Greer and his grandmother, Lolita Garcia, for igniting the spark that became this book. Lastly, we want to thank the staff of the Carnegie of Homestead - past, present, and future.

Table of Contents

Chapter 1
Running Late

An early morning sunbeam burst through the library window and landed on Liam.

The sunlight stirred him, and he slowly opened his eyes. He blinked a few times until his eyes adjusted to the morning light. He looked around the huge room in the library to check if anyone else was awake. Liam liked to wake up first. "I can enjoy the peace and quiet of the library before it gets busy," Liam thought. Another beautiful day at the Carnegie Library of Homestead!

Liam looked up at the big clock that hung above the main door and saw that it was twenty minutes to nine. "Miss Sperry is late," noticed Liam.

"She is always here by 8:30. I wonder what happened?" asked Liam.

The library opened at nine in the morning. Liam learned that by seeing where the big hand and the little one were on the clock face. He also knew six o'clock, where the long hand pointed straight up and the short hand pointed straight down. Liam knew that was closing time.

Miss Sperry was always on time and usually early. Just then, Liam heard the main door being unlocked. "She is here!" Liam shouted with joy.

The big wooden door opened, and in walked Miss Sperry, who didn't look very happy. "The trolley was fifteen minutes late," she muttered to herself. "Now I am going to have to rush around the library to get everything ready before I open."

Miss Sperry was the first librarian hired by the town of Homestead. She had worked at the library across the river in Braddock, and Mr. Carnegie wanted her to open his new library. Liam remembered hearing the opening ceremonies from his shelf. He heard the rain falling on the roof where a huge crowd of 1500 townspeople were gathered outside the library. He heard speeches from many important men. "I want to welcome our new librarian, Miss Sperry," remarked Mr. Carnegie. "Come on up to the podium and say a few words to the townspeople."

Miss Sperry walked up the steps and began to speak. Liam listened to her tell the townspeople her plans for the library. Liam didn't understand everything she wanted to do, but he got excited when she told them her plans for the children's room.

The crowd applauded at Miss Sperry's ideas for the new library. "Thank you, Mr. Carnegie. I am so proud to be the first librarian here at the Carnegie Library of Homestead," she said as she ended her talk and walked back to her seat. Mr. Carnegie invited the people to visit the new library before it officially opened on Saturday. This news got Liam very excited.

People could finally see him on the shelf and take him home.

One day, Liam heard sounds coming from the music hall.

Liam heard many instruments playing a song. He heard one of the patrons say that the song was called *The Carnegie Library March*, written by Charles Wakefield Cadman. Liam liked the song so much he began to move his pages to the beat of the music.

Liam remembered another day when Mr. Carnegie came into the library, and Miss Sperry almost fainted from all the excitement. Mr. Carnegie ran over to her and asked if she was alright. Miss Sperry looked up at him and said she was startled to see him enter the library. "I didn't mean to frighten you, but I wanted to see your improvements to our library. Would you show me around?" asked Mr. Carnegie.

"I would be honored," replied Miss Sperry. "Let me show you our children's room."

Liam watched them enter the room. "On the shelves to our left are the picture books for the little children. On the right are books for our older children and teenagers. I am letting the children browse through the books themselves." Miss Sperry explained. "I like the open stack idea, and I will suggest that the other libraries follow your lead," replied Mr. Carnegie.

Liam watched them walk out to the main room, where Miss Sperry showed him the holiday display.

"It's beautiful," exclaimed Mr. Carnegie. "Thank you," replied Miss Sperry. "I make a display for each month. Next month, I'm going to display books about our first president, George Washington."

"You keep up the great work," said Mr. Carnegie. "Next time I visit Pittsburgh, I will stop by and say hello."

"That would be very nice. You have a safe trip back to New York," said Miss Sperry. But Liam never saw Mr. Carnegie again.

Liam watched them say farewell and saw Mr. Carnegie walk out the front door. He liked that Miss Sperry waved goodbye.

Chapter 2

Nana's Story

Emily heated the water for Grandma's tea. Nana loved her tea, especially on cold winter days like today. Papa would get the coal stove going in a jiffy, and soon the kitchen would be warm and toasty.

The kitchen was Emily's favorite room in the house. She loved the smells and sounds of cooking and especially enjoyed baking with her Mama and Nana.

Since Pap passed away, Nana hardly left the kitchen. They had come to America together in 1885 from Hungary. They went through a waystation called Ellis on an island near New York City. From there, they lived with friends in Buffalo, and when Pap heard about the mill jobs in Homestead, he decided to take another leap of faith. They left everything behind, including loved ones, to start a new life in Pittsburgh.

Emily loved hearing Nana talk about their journey on a large boat where they stayed in a place called steerage. Nana recalled the experiences in vivid detail, so much so that Emily would find herself feeling seasick hearing about the storms and the smells and the spoiled food they were forced to eat. There was even a baby born during the trip, a boy they named Abraham, that Nana helped deliver.

Pap worked in the mill until he fell and broke his arm. After that, he tried to help in small ways, helping Nana around the house or bringing home a chicken for supper. Pap could fix anything and became the local handyman despite his broken arm.

Nana also remembered the big strike in 1892. Many men were hurt by the guards that the mill owners hired. Nana had little good to say about the owners. "Your Pap was there and saw it happen," recalled Nana. "And the men didn't get more money. Your Pap always said that the owners 'broke the backs' of the men." Emily didn't know what that meant, but she didn't like the mill owners. They seemed mean and selfish.

Emily's Papa worked at the mill, too. It was hard to make ends meet but the men were afraid to go on strike again, so they made due. Mama could make a meal from just about anything. Mama had a summer and winter garden. "We grow more than we need and preserve the rest," Mama explained. Emily loved canning days. So much activity and hustle and bustle with everyone working together. They grew cabbage, turnips, and squash in the winter and green beans, tomatoes, and onions in the summer. The summer garden fed them in the winter, and the winter garden fed them in the spring and early summer.

"Time for school," reminded Mama. Emily liked school and attended St. Mary's with her brother, Thomas. She liked math and science, but she liked English class the best. She was able to learn new words that she could teach Nana. And most important of all, she was able to read books. She and Tom bundled up and headed up the hill to school while Mama waved goodbye from the porch.

Chapter 3

A Visit from Mr. Washington

Liam had the perfect view to see all the happenings that went on in the library. He was on the third bookshelf, just high enough to see into the main room. He saw the workmen enter carrying their tools and fixing any problems in the library. But most of all, he could see if any children walked toward the children's reading room.

Liam recalled when a very important man came to visit the library. Liam remembered his name, Booker T. Washington, a college teacher from Alabama. He heard Miss Sperry welcome him to the library. Mr. Washington told Miss Sperry how beautiful the library was and how happy he was to see so many books for people to read. Liam heard Mr. Washington tell the crowd that, "The library is a special place for everyone to go and learn about the world." Liam listened to Mr. Washington say that he wished there had been a library for him when he was a child. He told the crowd that he wasn't allowed to use the library in his town because of the color of his skin. Mr. Washington explained, "This library is a special building where all are welcome." He gave Miss Sperry a copy of his book, *Up from Slavery,* and said he would be honored if she put it on the shelf for everyone to read. Miss Sperry thanked him for his donation and walked out the front door with him. The crowd followed behind and waved goodbye as Mr. Washington walked

down the stone steps.

Chapter 4

Lonesome Liam

Day after day, month after month, Liam stood upright on the shelf with all of the other books, waiting for a child to pick him up. Each day, he would watch the doors open and see the children come in and turn toward his section. Each day, he said to himself, "Today is the day I get picked to be brought home and read."

But no one ever picked Liam. Day after day, Liam patiently waited. Children would walk up and down the aisle looking at all the children's books. But they never chose Liam.

"I don't know what is wrong with me," Liam asked himself. "I'm a brand-new book. I have a new-book smell. My spine is strong, and my pages have never been turned. "Is it my title? Is it my pictures? Why can't I leave the library?" Liam was puzzled. Liam felt a tiny tear roll down his cover, leaving a sad stain.

Chapter 5
Friendly Faces

Liam was taking a nap when he heard the sound of footsteps coming down his aisle. He looked up to see a boy and girl looking at all the books. Liam started making funny noises to try to get their attention.

"Up here," Liam shouted to them. "Here I am. Pick me. I am a fantastic book to read!"

But the boy wandered over to the older children's books, and the girl started looking for picture books about animals. As she started getting closer to Liam, he felt his pages starting to shake. "She is three books from me," said Liam. "Now she is two books away. This could be the day," Liam thought to himself. Liam dreamed of going outside the library. He thought it was winter because the children wore hats and gloves. Liam didn't care if it was cold. He wanted so badly to go home with someone who wanted to open him and learn all about him.

The girl reached up to the bookshelf. Liam was so excited that his pages started flapping with anticipation. "C'mon, take me off the shelf!" exclaimed Liam.

But the girl selected the book about animals from Africa. As she pulled the book down from the shelf, Liam let out a scream. "Nooooooo!!! I'm the book you should read. I'm brand new and have lots of great pictures, too. I'm a much better book than him." The other book looked back at Liam and said, "Sorry, Liam, maybe next time."

"Yeah, maybe next time. That's all I ever hear. Next time," grumbled Liam. "Maybe today will never be the day."

Sadly, Liam went back to watching and hoping. Watching the front door for any child to come in and hoping one child would choose him.

During the afternoon, Liam watched many patrons come and go.

There was Mr. Kovechek, who owned the grocery store. He liked to read military books. Liam heard that he was with Teddy Roosevelt and his Roughriders in a place called San Juan.

In came Mrs. Lupinsky, who helped her husband run Lupinsky's Dry Goods. She liked to read historical romance novels. Liam saw her two boys run around the library chasing each other. Miss Sperry told them to stop and explained to them that libraries are quiet places. Mrs. Lupinsky apologized for her children's behavior. Miss Sperry told the boys to go over to the children's section. Turning to Mrs. Lupinsky, Miss Sperry smiled and said, "You have two good boys there. They are welcome back anytime."

Liam liked Miss Sperry. She would come over to his shelf and wipe away all of the dust that had gathered on the wooden shelf. She would straighten out the books and put them in their proper place.

Liam wished he had a family to go home to. "Someday, some little boy or girl will walk over, see me on the shelf, and reach for me. That will be the happiest day of my life," Liam thought.

Liam would watch the main door from his spot on the bookshelf. He would see the patrons come into the library and ask Miss Sperry for a book. She would direct them to the book's place in the library.

One day a family walked into the library. The husband was limping along using his wooden cane. His wife was watching him carefully to make sure he didn't fall. His children were trailing behind with a look of concern on their faces.

"Good morning, Mr. and Mrs. Lokich. And a very good morning to you children," said Miss Sperry.

"How are you feeling today Frank?"

"His leg is really bothering him because of the cold weather," replied Dolores Lokich.

"My daddy got hurt in the mill," piped up little Danny.

"I know," said Miss Sperry. "It's very sad that so many workers are getting hurt in the mill." Liam heard other boys talking about the dangers of working in the steel mills. Liam didn't understand why men would want to work in a place so dangerous.

Chapter 6

Miss Sperry to The Rescue

"Oh no!" Liam exclaimed. "Here comes Billy Wilson and his younger brother, Butch. The last time they were here, Miss Sperry scolded them for making too much noise and even threatened to take away their library cards. Liam watched the brothers start to walk to the children's section. Miss Sperry kept her watchful eye on them.

As Billy passed by the front desk, he said softly, "Good day, Miss Sperry." "Good day back to you boys," Miss Sperry replied. "You boys behave now," reminded Miss Sperry. "We will," Billy said back as he winked at his younger brother.

Liam saw that wink from Billy and knew there would be trouble. "I'm going to keep a close watch on those two," Liam thought to himself as they wandered around the children's section. Liam remembered the last time Billy and his brother came into the library and ran around the room, pulling books off the shelf, and talking loudly. One time, Liam saw Billy take a crayon out of his pocket and scribble in a book. Liam was worried that they might do something bad to him or the other books.

"I'm getting one of these picture books about animals and stuff," Butch told his brother.

"Yeah, me too," said Billy. Liam watched them very carefully to see what book they would choose.

"I'm taking this one," said Billy. "It's all about poisonous snakes."

"I'm going to find me a good one, too," exclaimed Butch as he stood right in front of Liam.

Butch reached up with his right hand and went straight to Liam.

"This is it," thought Liam. "He is picking me."

Butch took Liam off the shelf.

Butch held Liam in his hand as he walked over to the table and sat down with his brother.

"What's it about?" asked Billy.

"I don't know, but I am going find out," answered Butch.

Liam was so excited. He was off the shelf for the first time in his life. He felt his spine stretch as Butch opened him and looked at his pictures. Butch quickly skimmed through the pages of the book.

"This book is so dopey! There are no good pictures of scary stuff. I don't want this book."

"Look at this picture," Butch said to his brother as he held up Liam for Billy to see.

"You're right," said Billy. "It's a silly picture book."

"I'll make sure no one takes this book out of the library," said Butch.

"What are you going to do?" asked Billy.

"Just watch," said Butch.

"Oh no!" thought Liam. "What is he going to do to me?"

Butch looked over his shoulder and located Miss Sperry. She was sitting behind the front counter. "Good." said Butch. "She can't see me."

Liam watched Butch bring both hands to the top of his cover and begin to tear.

"Owww!" screamed Liam. "You are hurting me. Stop. Please stop."

But Butch ripped Liam's cover in half.

"There," said Butch. "Now, no one will want this book."

Billy looked up from his picture book and saw what Butch had done.

"You shouldn't have ripped the cover," said Billy. "Let's get out of here before Miss Sperry sees what you did."

"Yeah," said Butch. "Let's scram."

The boys left Liam on the table with his cover torn in half. "Help me!" cried Liam. "My cover is torn. I need to go to the library hospital."

The brothers saw that Miss Sperry was busy with a patron, so they snuck right past her.

"Someone help me," Liam quietly moaned. "My cover needs fixed. Someone help me. Please!!!"

Liam watched the kids come and go from the children's room. Not one child stopped to help Liam, no matter how much he cried out for help.

"No one stopped to help me," Liam said to himself. "I will never get to the library hospital."

Around closing time, Miss Sperry walked into the children's section and spotted Liam on the table.

"What happened to you, my little guy?" she thought to herself. "Who could have torn this cover in half?"

Liam looked up through his watery, tear-stained eyes and said, "Help me, please, Miss Sperry."

Miss Sperry picked up Liam gently and took him to the front of the library. She walked behind the counter and sat down at her desk. "I need to repair the cover on this book, but I don't have time," Miss Sperry said to herself. "I don't want to miss my trolley."

She reached down into the bottom desk drawer and pulled out a plain brown book cover.

"This will have to do until I can repair the cover tomorrow."

Liam breathed a sigh of relief as Miss Sperry removed the torn cover and began putting the new cover around him.

"That feels so much better," Liam said.

"I feel like a brand-new book again. Now, someone for sure will take me home," said Liam hopefully. Liam was so grateful. He knew Miss Sperry was a good librarian. He knew she cared about him and the other books.

"Oh my. Look at the time. I need to close the library," said Miss Sperry as she returned Liam to his place on the shelf and walked back out of the children's room. Liam watched as Miss Sperry checked the library for patrons. She turned out the lights and walked out the front door. Liam heard her lock the door. Neither Miss Sperry nor Liam realized that she forgot to put his title on the cover. Now, he would be even more invisible.

"It's all quiet now," sighed Liam. "Maybe tomorrow, someone will take me home."

Chapter 7
The Castle on The Hill

Emily and Thomas were excited to open their gifts on Christmas morning. Neither expected much more than a small toy and maybe an orange and some candy or nuts. Papa and Mama sat watching them open their gifts with a sense of anticipation. What the children didn't know was that Mama, Papa, and Nana had been saving for months to make this Christmas special. It was the first since Pap died, so last year's holiday was colored with sadness.

Thomas' gift was a used red bicycle that Papa had restored. It was the first bike that Thomas had ever owned. He was so excited that he wanted to take it outside for a ride. "There is snow on the ground, so you can't ride it today," explained Papa.

Emily opened her gift excitedly.

When she saw the coat, she started to weep. It was the exact same coat that she had admired at Lupinsky's on Eighth Avenue. She remembered her mother saying they couldn't afford such a coat, and Emily quickly forgot about it, although she still went down to the store to admire it in the window until it was taken down in November. She had wondered what lucky little girl would think of such a grand present.

Emily tried on the coat. "It fits perfectly," Papa commented, "It should last you at least two years, but then you are growing up so fast." Mama added, "Emily, you can wear your new coat when you and Thomas go to the library tomorrow."

Emily had never been to the new library on the hill. To her, it looked like a castle. As Emily and Thomas walked up the steep hill to the library, Emily turned to Thomas and said, "I'm so excited to see the inside of the library."

Thomas replied, "I can't wait to see the swimming pool. I'm taking my first swimming lesson."

As they entered, Thomas headed towards the door to the Athletic Club, and Emily opened the main door to the library. As she entered, she immediately noticed how much bigger it looked inside. She also saw a friendly face, Miss Sperry. Emily remembered how Miss Sperry came down to the 5th Ward with books, but they weren't always the ones she wanted. She had read *Little Women* and *Alice in Wonderland*, but she wanted a book about real things.

Miss Sperry welcomed her and showed her to the children's room. It was bright, with tall ceilings and large windows that let in natural light. She could see the dust motes dancing in the cool sunshine that streamed through the windows.

But more importantly, she noticed that the room contained dozens and dozens and dozens of books.

Chapter 8
Today's the Day

The sound of the library door opening stirred Liam. He blinked his eyes a few times as Miss Sperry turned on the lights. "I feel today is the day that I get to go out of the library," Liam thought to himself. "A nice warm home where someone will open my pages and enjoy looking at my pictures. If I keep saying to myself over and over, 'Today is the day,' then it will happen. This is my magic phrase."

Liam watched Miss Sperry get the library ready for the day and all of the activities in the many rooms. Liam watched as she swept the floor and dusted the bookshelves. Liam felt very sure that today would be special. He didn't know why, exactly, but he felt it with each passing minute.

Later in the morning, a group of neighborhood kids came in. Liam saw Miss Sperry bring her index finger up to her mouth to signal to the children to stay quiet. Liam knew it was Saturday. Liam loved Saturdays. It was the busiest day of the week in the children's section. He knew the children were very excited to be out of school for the weekend. Liam saw many boys and girls with wet hair coming into the library. Liam heard one of the boys say that the swimming pool was a lot of fun and he was learning to swim. Miss Sperry came into the room and told all the children to find seats. The children were excited for story time. Miss Sperry read an adventure story called *The Odyssey*. Liam liked the story because it had a monster with one eye. The children sat quietly as Miss Sperry read the story. When she was finished, Miss Sperry told the children they could get a book to take home.

Liam watched with hopeful eyes. "Come on over," Liam tried to yell, but no one heard him. "Maybe if I rustle my pages, that will get their attention."

Liam shook his pages back and forth and called out as loudly as he could. A little brown-haired girl in a blue coat heard the noise from Liam and walked over to his shelf. "Did I hear a book make a noise?" she asked herself. She looked back and forth at the row of books until she stopped at Liam. "What is this book about?" she said. "There is no title on the cover." Even Liam didn't know his own title. A book must be read by a child at least once. That is how books learn about themselves.

All of a sudden, Liam started to get excited. "Today is the day!" shouted Liam. "She is picking me!" Liam trembled with excitement as he watched the brown-haired girl in the blue coat.

The little girl reached up and took Liam down from the shelf. She looked at the cover with no title and wondered what the book was about. She went over and sat down at the wooden table and opened Liam. She looked at the first two pages and began to smile. "This is the book I want," she said to herself. Liam got so excited when the girl got up from the desk and walked over to the counter to see Miss Sperry. "I want to check out this book," the little girl said to Miss Sperry. Liam started to shake; he was so excited. "Today is the day I get to go outside," exclaimed Liam.

"Here is my library card," the little girl said to Miss Sperry. "Thank you, Emily, and here is the book. Be careful with it because it doesn't have its original cover." "I will," said Emily. "I'll be extra careful because this is a special book." "Remind me to put a new cover on your book when you return it," said Miss Sperry. "I will," replied Emily.

"You have three weeks before you need to return it," Miss Sperry reminded the little girl. "I'll remember," Emily answered as she walked out of the library with Liam. Emily couldn't see, but Liam had a great big smile on his cover.

Emily skipped down the stone steps of the library. She turned left and walked down the sidewalk. "I can't wait to show my mama and papa what I found," she exclaimed.

Chapter 9

Home at Last

Emily walked down Margaret Street to her rowhouse near the mill. She ran up the steps to her porch, opened the door, and shouted, "I'm home."

"Come in here and sit with your papa and show me what book you got at the library," said her father.

Emily's dad was home because the mill workers were on strike. "Are you ever going back to work?" Emily asked her papa.

"Soon, I hope. We want them to pay us a living wage," explained Papa. "Then we will go back."

"I don't like you being on strike. That's why I got this book to help cook in the kitchen with Mama," Emily said to Papa.

Emily sat down in the green upholstered chair and started to open Liam.

"Oh, Papa," said Emily. "This is the perfect book for me. There was no title on the cover, so I didn't know what the book was about. But when I opened it and saw the pictures, I knew it was the right book for me."

"Well," Papa replied with a wink. "You should never judge a book by its cover."

"What does that mean?" asked Emily.

Papa explained to Emily that the old saying meant that you shouldn't judge someone or something like your book based only on what you see on the outside or what you think without knowing the full story.

Emily thought for a minute about what her papa told her. "I still don't understand, Papa," said Emily. Papa looked at Emily and explained, "Do you remember when Mama made perogies and sauerkraut for Nana's birthday? You said the sauerkraut looked like cooked worms and you didn't want to eat it. But Nana said try some and you tasted it and you liked it. That's an example of what the saying means. Now take your book into the kitchen and show Mama and Nana."

Emily closed Liam and took him into the kitchen to introduce him to Mama and Nana. "Look!" Emily excitedly said. "This is the book that will help me make wonderful meals for us. It has recipes for dinners and desserts like cakes and pies."

"Let me see your book," Mama asked Emily.

Emily handed her Mama the book, and Mama opened Liam.

"It has beautiful pictures of the fruits and vegetables we can use in our meals," Emily told Mama. "We can try to make one of the recipes for beef stew from the book."

Liam was so happy when he found out he was a recipe book for children. He could hardly keep from rustling his pages, he was so excited.

Emily sat at the kitchen table and continued to look at the different types of fruits and vegetables.

"What is this fruit?" Emily asked her Mama. "I have never seen this one before."

Emily showed her Mama the picture of the fruit.

"That is a mango, Emily," Mama told her. "They don't grow here in Homestead."

Emily looked in the back of Liam and found some easy recipes.

"Can you teach me to make an apple pie?" Emily asked her Mama.

"There is a recipe in the back. Does Papa like apple pie?"

"It's his favorite. Let's make it for his birthday next week," said Mama.

"We can go to the fruit market and pick out the most delicious apples for Papa's birthday pie," added Nana.

Mama and Emily didn't notice that Liam had a wide grin on his front cover. This was the happiest day of Liam's life.

Later that night, when it was time for bed, Emily took Liam upstairs to her room.

She lit her oil lamp, lay down in her bed, and opened Liam.

"I am so happy to have found this book so I can help Mama cook and make desserts for Papa," Emily said quietly.

Liam heard every word she said. This is what Liam had hoped for all those months of waiting on the bookshelf.

"Time to go to sleep," Mama said as she walked into Emily's bedroom.

Mama bent down and kissed Emily on her forehead. "Good night, sweetie. See you in the morning."

"Good night, Mama," answered Emily.

Mama turned off the lamp and walked out of the bedroom.

Emily closed Liam and placed him on her chest to hold for the night.

Liam had never felt so much love in his life. "This is the best I could have ever hoped for," Liam said.

"I have finally become a real book after waiting all this time," Liam whispered.

Liam closed his eyes and went to sleep, knowing that he was home, and he was loved.

THE END